A GUIDE TO WALKING HADRIAN'S WALL

by
Graham Mizon

First Edition, April 1977
Second Impression, April 1979
Third Impression, April 1983
Fourth Impression, February 1987
Fifth Impression, March 1990
Revised Edition, May 1993

Published by: Hendon Publishing Co. Ltd., Hendon Mill, Nelson, Lancashire.
Text © Graham Mizon, 1977
Printed by: Peter Fretwell & Sons Ltd., Healey Works, Goulbourne Street, Keighley, West Yorkshire BD21 1PZ.

The Seventeen Roman Forts

ENGLISH NAME	ROMAN NAME	ACRES
Wallsend	Segedunum	4
Newcastle	Pons Aelius	?
Benwell	Condercum	5·64
Rudchester	Vindovala	4·5
Halton Chesters	Onnum	4·8
*Chesters	Cilurnum	5·75
Carrawbrough	Brocolitia	3·5
*Housesteads	Vercovicium	5
*Chesterholm	Nindolanda	3·5
Great Chesters	Aesica	3
Carvoran	Banna	4
Birdoswald	Camboglanna	5·33
Castlesteads	Uxellodunum	3·75
Stanwix	Petriana	9·32
Burgh by Sands	Aballava	4·75
Drumburg	Congavata	?
Bowness	Maia	7

*Museums

This book is in memory of Eirwyn Morgan Davies, who first taught me to love the country.

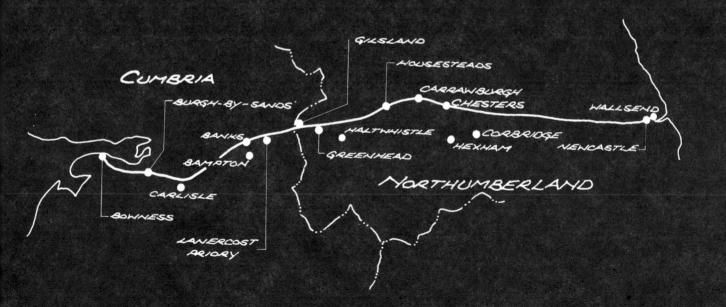

Above: The Wall at Walltown Crags
(Photo. by Colin Walker—Pendyke Publications)

About this book

From the time of Bede (A.D. 731) to the present day, people have walked, and been fascinated by, Hadrian's Wall. The most remarkable walker was the Antiquary, William Hutton, who at the age of 78 walked from Birmingham to Hadrian's Wall, along it twice and back home; a round trip of 601 miles. He wrote of his experiences in a book called *The History of the Roman Wall*, published in 1802. He laughingly writes, 'What can exceed the folly of that man, who, at seventy-eight, walked six hundred miles to see a shattered Wall!'

Today, much of that 'shattered Wall' is cared for by the English Heritage, which has restored and excavated much of it. It stretches 73½ miles from the Tyne to the Solway coast, but only 10 miles of that carries any evidence of the Wall.

This book is an attempt to guide you from coast to coast taking in all the worth while places to visit. We have a rich variety of walking, from high ridges to cultivated plains, but the Wall is known by many to pass through some of Britain's loveliest scenery.

Unlike the Pennine Way, Hadrian's Wall is not a long distance footpath, which means that we are found swerving from our course from time to time. Generally a compass is not essential, but the Ordnance Survey map of Hadrian's Wall is invaluable. Most people do not attempt to walk its whole length, and this book is designed in such a way that you can pick it up at any point on the walk. I have followed the pattern of my predecessors in that I have worked from east to west so as to take in the turrets and milecastles in numerical order. With interpretation, however, you can use this book whilst walking in either direction.

At the commencement of each chapter a simple sketch-map has been included which can be related to the subsequent text; it is not, however, drawn to scale.

With a map in one hand and this guide in the other, you will, I hope, gain all that Hadrian's Wall has to offer the walker. If this is achieved, I will feel that this venture has been worthwhile.

Graham Mizon, May 1993.

About Hadrian ... and his wall

Hadrian was born in A.D.76, and he grew up at a small town called Italica in Spain. At the age of 10, his father died and the boy was cared for by a relative called Trajan, who in the year A.D.98 became Emperor of Rome.

Trajan was an enthusiastic emperor and involved his country in many wars. It was during a war in the Middle East that Trajan was taken ill and later died. His widow immediately proclaimed Hadrian as successor.

Hadrian was a very different man, and he soon made peace with many lands including the Middle East countries, and the taxes came down in Rome as war expenses were not as high.

He looked upon his job as being a peacemaker, and his visit to Britain was highly successful, as he made sure that taxes were fairly paid. So the Britons accepted the Roman Government and respected Hadrian. They were, however, continually troubled by raiders from the north, so Hadrian launched a mammoth campaign to build a frontier to deter the barbarians.

And so in the year A.D.122, Hadrian walked the country and planned a course, although he never stayed to see it through. Today this mighty work bears the Emperor's name, and, although the Wall has been unoccupied for some 15 centuries, many remains are still evident.

We are not employed in walking a Wall, but a **fortification;** a Roman frontier with many structures. They comprise the Wall, a Ditch, the Vallum, Mile-castles, Turrets and Forts.

The Wall was built 80 Roman (73½ English) miles long, from Wallsend on the River Tyne, to Bowness on Solway. Its height was around 15ft., with a 6ft. parapet on top. The thickness varies from place to place. The original plan was to build the Wall at 10 Roman feet wide, known now as the Broad Wall, but later a new instruction came to build the Wall at a narrower gauge of 8 Roman feet.

At places you can see where the Romans had already built the broad foundation, and then built the Narrow Wall on top of it. Once the Romans crossed the River Irthing into Cumberland, however, there was a shortage of limestone, so they built the Wall with turf and timber, although the stone Wall soon replaced it.

The Ditch was an extra defence line which ran 20 feet north of the Wall. It was 27ft. wide and 9ft. deep. Where the Wall climbs up the crags, the ditch was not dug as the high ground was ample protection.

The Vallum is a ditch larger than the previous one, and lying south of the Wall. There is a ditch 20ft. wide at the top and 8ft. wide at the bottom, with a mound on either side of it.

Its use has been questioned, but it does act as the southern demarcation line of the Roman frontier.

Milecastles were small quarters, normally built every Roman mile (1620 yards). The interior varies considerably in size, but on average is 20 by 25 yards. Apart from living accommodation they also served as an observation post and customs point.

Turrets are 20ft. square towers, two of which were equally spaced between the milecastles. Turrets are usually partly recessed into the Wall, and the door is situated on the south side.

Forts were rectangular shaped buildings with rounded edges, rather like the shape of a playing card. Some are recessed into the Wall as at Housesteads, others have their northern third projecting through the Wall, as at Chesters. There are also some which are not even on the line of the Wall, as at Vindolanda and Castlesteads.

There are 17 forts, all of different sizes and names: **(See list on page 2)**

Today there are museums to be found at Chesters, Housesteads and Vindolanda, and admission charges to the forts apply at Chesters, Housesteads, Vindolanda and Birdoswald.

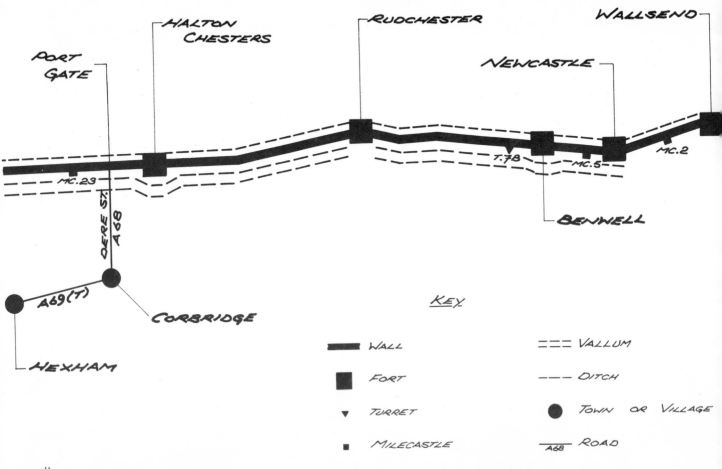

PORT GATE

HALTON CHESTERS

RUDCHESTER

WALLSEND

NEWCASTLE

MC.23

DERE ST. A68

T.7B

MC.5

MC.2

BENWELL

A69(T)

CORBRIDGE

HEXHAM

KEY

▬▬▬ WALL

◼ FORT

▼ TURRET

▪ MILECASTLE

═══ VALLUM

––– DITCH

● TOWN OR VILLAGE

A68 ROAD

1. Wallsend - Hexham

Wallsend: It would be nice to see a large fort or a great chunk of the Wall to indicate the start of Hadrian's Wall, but no such landmark is visible. In fact nothing remains between here and Newcastle, a distance of $3\frac{1}{2}$ miles.

I walked from Wallsend Station down to Buddle Street, the site of the first fort on the Wall. The town council have just cleared the site of Buddle Street for re-development, and have put their planning back to allow the Department of the Environment to come in and seize the opportunity to excavate. The Corporation have also outlined the limits of the fort with white lines in the roads. I found some in the neighbouring streets off Buddle Street, but they are not easy to find.

Segedunum, the Roman name for Wallsend Fort, was 4 acres with 4 double gates, the eastern gateway being on the site of Simpson's Hotel. The building of the fort and the Wall took place at a later stage, as excavations have shown that the Wall was built at the Narrow Gauge (7ft. 6ins. thick on a 8ft. foundation), which was only introduced during the second phase of planning.

We will now follow as near as we can the line of the Wall. Going west down Buddle Street, follow the A187 which leads onto the Fossway. Along Fossway the line of the Wall is to the right and joins us where the fire station lies. About a quarter of a mile down the road we arrive at the Fosse Public House on the junction of Roman Avenue, which stands on the site of Milecastle 2. Follow the Fossway a further $\frac{1}{2}$ mile, which leads up to Byker Hill, along the Shields Road and into Newcastle.

Newcastle: The exact line of the Wall is not certain through Newcastle, although it has been detected from St. Dominic's Church to Sallyport Gate. The Romans built their second fort here which is also undefined, but it was known to be called Pons Aelius, meaning Hadrian's Bridge. The bridge referred to here stood on the grounds of the present Swing Bridge.

Despite no remains in the centre of Newcastle, the city houses one of the best Roman exhibitions in the country. Of great interest is a reproduction of a Mithras Temple with taped commentary. The museum is situated in the University grounds.

Benwell: The Wall continues west out of Newcastle along the Westgate Road north of the Central Station. The road rises up Arthur's Hill, and Milecastle 5 stood near the cemetery which is seen before reaching the summit.

We pass the General Hospital and enter Benwell (about 2 miles out of Newcastle) which boasts a Roman Temple. The route is well signposted and leads you down Weidner Road opposite a school. Take the first right (Westholme Gardens) and first left (Broomridge Avenue) and the Temple will be seen on the left. It is attractive and kept neat by the Department of the Environment, although the altars are casts from the originals. It is certainly worth a visit as it is the only structure visible of the Benwell Fort (Condercum) meaning 'the place with a good look-out'. It is set upon a 415ft. hill and commands the surrounding area, particularly to the south.

200 yards west of this site lies the remains of the only Vallum Crossing to be seen today along the whole line of the Wall. The access is from the main West Road, turning down Denhill Park. Unlike the previous site there are no signposts leading to it. At the foot of Denhill Park the Crossing can be seen. It is kept under lock and key, and the latter is obtainable from 65 Denhill Park. The whole site is quite impressive with the west pier still in its original position.

Denton: Continuing along West Road (A69), we descend to a roundabout at Denton Burn. Just beyond this on the left we hit gold, the first piece of Wall to be seen from the east! It was excavated in 1927, and is the Broad Wall on a clay foundation.

A little farther down the road are two more sections and in better condition, the second piece containing the first visible Turret, 7b Denton Hall. Excavated in 1929, it stands 4ft. high and again is well preserved by the Department of the Environment.

It is rather encouraging to the Wall walker to see these stretches of Wall, as until now it has taken some imagination to believe that you are actually walking in the footsteps of the Romans.

Continuing along the road, we arrive at West Denton where the A69 becomes the A69(T) which routes traffic around Corbridge and Hexham. When the roundabout is reached go left up the sliproad and take the B6528, following the Wall through Blutcher to Throckley. Despite no Wall to interest the walker, there are along here fine views of the Tyne Valley to the South. It was at Throckley in 1879 that a discovery of some 5,000 silver coins was made.

Heddon on the Wall: Leaving Throckley and the county of Tyne and Wear, we enter the first village in Northumberland, Heddon on the Wall. On the south side of the road is a well preserved 100 yard stretch of the Wall. It is the Broad Wall and stands up to 7 courses high. At the western end is an unusual circular structure which is not thought to be Roman.

Apart from the Wall little is worth seeing in Heddon, and so we leave by the B6318 signposted 'Chollerford' and 'Roman Wall'. The road is built on the Wall, and so we follow exactly the line until the A69(T) interrupts again and forces upon us a ¼ mile detour. The bypass has been built taking little care for the walker. The only consolation is that our crossing is well signposted, and soon we are far from the boom of the traffic and again following the Wall along the so called 'Military Road'.

Rudchester: The road rises to a crossroads where the ditch (to the north) and the Vallum (to the south) can be seen en-route. Just after the junction is the site of the fourth fort on the Wall, Rudchester, the modern name

Right: Walltown Crags, looking east, as it may have appeared in Hadrian's day. Drawing by Alan Sorrel. (Crown Copyright, reproduced with permission of the Controller of Her Majesty's Stationery Office.)

for Vindovala. Apart from a farm called Rudchester there is nothing to suggest that a fort ever existed here. Old William Hutton in 1801 on arriving here claimed, 'I have all along inquired for turrets; but might as well have inquired among the stars'.

Rudchester once covered 4½ acres and commanded the March Burn Valley. In the Newcastle Museum there is a life-size statue of Hercules which was excavated here around 1760.

Between Rudchester and the next fort, Halton Chesters, (a distance of 7½ miles) there is no Wall to excite the eye, although better views of the Vallum and the ditch can be seen. It was on this stretch that I foolishly turned down the offer of a lift. Walking is not pleasant here, and I was looking forward to the time when I could rid myself of the road. We are fortunate today, however, as the bypass mentioned earlier, has at least taken most of the heavy traffic off this once heavily used road.

Halton Chesters: Halton Chesters, like Rudchester, holds no visible remains and lies ¾ mile east of Dere Street, which passes through the Wall at Port Gate. Dere Street, which is now the A68, leads to the Corstopitum Roman Station at Corbridge for which we shall now head. The 2½ mile walk down the A68 didn't sound inviting, and so from Halton Chesters I found a lovely country walk to Corbridge taking in two post-Roman castles.

On the site of Halton Chesters are two pillars and a small lane running between them. The lane leads to Halton Castle, the home today of Major Blackett. The Carnaby family used to reside here in the middle ages, but only London's Carnaby Street remembers them today. Passing the castle there is a fork in the lane. Take the right hand one which leads to another fork. This time take the left turning which descends to Aydon Castle. The walk is really beautiful and a welcome change from the Military Road. Aydon Castle is in a state of ruin and supported by wooden blocks. Even so it is impressive, and the atmosphere of the place is quite enchanting.

From the castle go through a white gate where a footpath takes you through a delightful wood. At the end we meet face to face with the enemy—the A69(T). Because of the intrusion we have to turn left to the B6321, going over the bridge and turning up the opposite bank of the bypass—and so enter Corbridge down a lane.

Corbridge: Before seeking the Roman Station the town itself is worth looking at. In the Market Place is St. Andrew's Church, a beautiful Saxon structure. In the lower part of the west end tower is a porch which was built out of Roman stones from Corstopitum. The Vicar's Pele, dated late 13th century, today houses the Tourist Information Centre. Outside the Pele is the Market Cross which originally stood on a Roman altar in the Market Place, now replaced by the Percy Cross dated 1814—a gift of the Duke of Northumberland.

Corstopitum lies ½ mile west of its English successor, and signposts lead you along Watling Street and Roman

Way to the car park entrance. It was built before the Wall, probably under Agricola, although later many structural alterations were made. It was ideally situated at the junction of the Stanegate and Dere Street at an easy crossing of the Tyne. The station remained unoccupied for a time until Hadrian arrived and used it as a supply base. Later, however, more forts were built on the Wall and Corstopitum was once more evacuated.

There is much to see on the site, in particular the granaries and the impressive colonnade. There are also remains of a fountain and water tank. There are temples, officers' quarters and a large store-house to be seen. The museum is small and quaint and full of interesting finds, including the famous Corbridge Lion.

Hexham: 3 miles due west of Chollerford lies the beautiful town of Hexham. Unlike Corbridge it cannot boast any Roman settlement, although a few Roman remains have been found. Hexham is worth a visit as it is an 'old world' town affected little by modern planning. It is situated on a shelf overlooking the River Tyne and is well positioned on good vantage roads.

The centre of attraction is Hexham Abbey. St. Wilfrid was the founder in A.D. 674, but most of the present building was restored in 1113. Christian people continue to gather here to worship each week, continuing the tradition of those people of long ago and yet witnessing to a Christ who is the same today as then. By the west door is a Saxon Font which was made from the base of a Roman pillar. One of the best sights is that of the Rood Screen, reputed to be one of the finest pieces of woodwork in England.

Hexham also has a very good Market Place and quaint shops; or for those who wish to escape humanity, the town is favoured with some lovely open spaces, none more beautiful than the Priory Grounds.

However, we must take our leave of Hexham and join again the line of Hadrian's Wall, continuing westwards towards our goal: the Wall Country.

Overleaf: (left) Corstopitum Roman Station near Corbridge. This photograph shows the eastern granary. Beneath the ground were channels so that air could circulate to keep the corn dry. (Newcastle Chronicle and Journal.)

Overleaf (right) Corstopitum Roman Station near Corbridge. The Colonnade on the main Stanegate Road south of the granaries. (Crown Copyright, reproduced with permission of the Controller of Her Majesty's Stationery Office.)

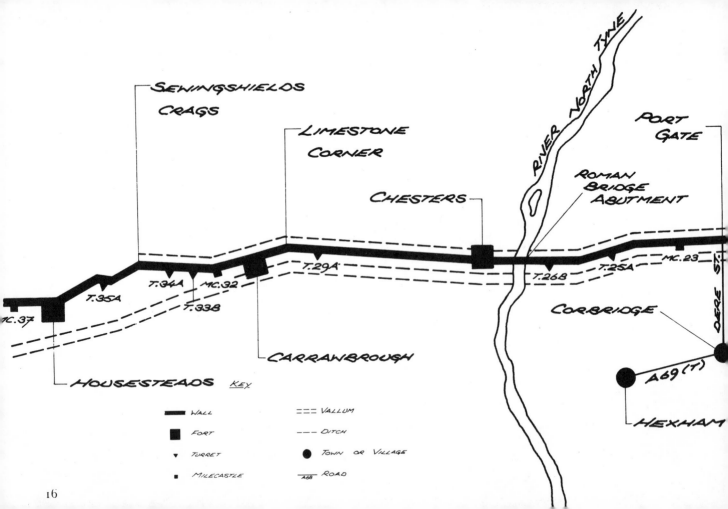

SEWINGSHIELDS CRAGS

LIMESTONE CORNER

CHESTERS

RIVER NORTH TYNE

PORT GATE

ROMAN BRIDGE ABUTMENT

T.29A

T.26B T.25A MC.23

T.35A T.34A MC.32

T.33B

DERE ST.

CORBRIDGE

MC.37

CARRAWBROUGH

A69 (T)

HOUSESTEADS Key

HEXHAM

▬▬	WALL	≡≡≡	VALLUM
■	FORT	– – –	DITCH
▼	TURRET	●	TOWN OR VILLAGE
▪	MILECASTLE	‾A68‾	ROAD

2. Port Gate - Housesteads

Port Gate: Port Gate is the name given to the crossroads just west of Halton Chesters. Here there was a gate in the Wall for the Roman road of Dere Street to pass through. From here we head westwards along the B6318, walking once more the line of the Wall.

Along this next stretch the ditch is very prominent and makes up for any lack of Wall. I was looking forward to Milecastle 23 which the Ordnance map indicates as being identifiable, bearing in mind that we haven't yet seen a single milecastle. However, the find was disappointing. If you have a good eye you will detect a grass mound in the field south of the road. I thought it was hardly worth a black mark on the map, and I left still admiring the ditch and the Vallum.

At Hill Head, on the site of Turret 25a, the road bears south leaving the Wall running some 50 yards away in a field north of the road. Above the Wall is St. Oswald's Church, and by the road is a wooden cross, the original of which King Oswald erected to commemorate the battle of Heavenfield in A.D. 635.

Brunton: Pass Planetrees Farm on the south of the road where it bends back to the line of the Wall, for here we have a fine section of Wall about 50 yards long. This stretch has caused some head-scratching as at one end it is at the usual Broad Gauge and at the other it is only 6ft. wide, less than the standard Narrow Gauge.

A 1 in 10 decline to Lower Brunton takes us away from the Wall again; this time we head north whilst the Wall goes through a wooded area on its way to Chesters Fort. There is a piece of Wall in this section but we can only gain lawful access from the Hexham Road. So continue down the hill until a crossroads is reached. Turn left down the A6079 signposted 'Hexham' and the Wall will be seen 200 yards on the left. Climb over the stile and up the hill. This is a very important section as it is the highest stretch of Broad Wall to be seen today and contains perhaps the best turret on the Wall: 26b Brunton Turret. It was excavated in 1863 and the north wall stands today 11 courses high.

Roman Bridge Abutment: The Wall continues west on the opposite side of the road leading down to the River North Tyne, but none of it is evident today apart from the Roman Bridge Abutment.

To gain access we have to re-track to the Lower Brunton Crossroads described above. Turn left to Chollerford. Just before the bridge over the river, there is a gate on the left which leads to the Bridge Abutment. It is a good 1 mile round trip, but certainly worth the effort. Here are the remains of a bridge that once carried the Wall over to Chesters Fort. It is very impressive with huge stones. The Wall is Narrow on Broad and runs into a tower 22ft. square. The bridge was later altered when the Military Way was built. The river has changed its course since Roman times which means that although the Abutment is clear on this side, on the other bank nothing remains.

Chesters Fort: Back on the road at Chollerford, go

over the bridge and take the B6318 to Chesters Fort about half a mile west of the bridge. The Romans called the fort Cilurnum and built it on a natural shelf above the river in order to free it from the possibility of flooding. It is larger than the previous forts on the Wall, covering 5¾ acres. It is beautifully situated in the North Tyne Valley, with Warden Hill to the south and Walwick and Fallowfield Fells to the west and east. As a fort it didn't really serve as a control tower, as it could only command the view north along the valley. Perhaps the fort was purposely built in a sheltered position in an area where water was easily and quickly available. Its main purpose was as a Cavalry Fort, and it is the best example of such within the Roman Empire.

The highlight of Chesters is the Bath House situated outside the walls of the fort down by the river. Apart from the main structures which, are striking, there is a remarkable amount of detail evident such as the stoke-hole and the main drain. Chesters is also fortunate in having an excellent museum, chock-a-block with Roman stones, inscriptions, tombstones and the like. Also there are showcases full of tools, coins and odds and ends found during excavations. There are also light refreshments available on the site.

Black Carts: The line of the Wall west of the fort

Left: Brunton Turret (26b) excavated in 1863. The north wall, standing 11 courses high can be seen, with the doorway to the south. (Ian Penney.)

goes through private ground, and so for 500 yards we lose the Wall. Going out of the main entrance of the fort, turn left and the road rises to Walwick. The line of the Wall soon joins us, being the Narrow Wall on Broad Foundation. The road takes 2 miles to climb out of the valley, and looking back we have panoramic views to the south-east. At the crest of the hill we look down on to two fine stretches of Wall, and enter into the first of 398 square miles of the Northumberland National Park.

Access to the first stretch is gained by walking past the Wall and turning up a lane, where stepping stones lead over a wall and into the field containing the Wall and a fine turret: 29a Black Carts. The former is a good example of the Narrow on Broad type and is 200 yards long, standing 5 courses high in places. The turret, which was excavated fully in 1912, stands 11 courses high on the north, but only the bottom course remains of the south side. At a glance it looks like a cross section of a turret purposely designed for us to peep into. The hardest task when looking at these square foundations is trying to picture them at full height with a roof on.

Leaving the field where we entered there are stepping stones built into a wall on the opposite side of the lane to gain access to the second piece of Wall. This is also well preserved and set in mortar.

Limestone Corner: To save walking along the road again I left the Wall, following the ditch which is very marked here. I wanted to head for Limestone Corner where the Romans had difficulty digging the ditch.

Left: Chesters Fort, part of the Commandant's House. Crown Copyright, reproduced with permission of the Controller of Her Majesty's Stationery Office.)

Right: Chesters Fort, the changing rooms in the Bath House. (Ian Penny.)

Once submerged in the ditch you are in a world of your own. I could well imagine school children being caught up by the atmosphere and playing 'Romans and Picts'.

On its way to Limestone Corner, the ditch leads past an Ordnance Survey Triangulation Station, the northernmost part of Hadrian's Wall, and for a time of the Roman Empire. It was here that the Romans ran the ditch through very hard quartz dolerite, or so they tried. There are still many boulders remaining on the north lip, and a very large rock estimated at weighing 13 tons, lying in the ditch. In the top of this rock you can clearly see the wedge marks where they had tried to break it up.

Carrawbrough: From Limestone Corner we are reluctantly brought back onto the road. We have fine views in all directions, and good stretches of the ditch and Vallum.

4 miles west of Chollerford we arrive at Carrawbrough (pronounced Carrawbruff), the 7th fort on the Wall. A signpost 200 yards before the site reads 'Brocolitia' which is the Latin name for the fort. Carrawbrough (as we shall call it) was $3\frac{1}{2}$ acres and lay completely south of the Wall, being built over the course of the Vallum.

After Chesters, the fort proves disappointing with only the ramparts showing vaguely the outline. Outside the line of the fort, however, lies Carrawbrough's treasure: a Mithras Temple. A path from the car park leads directly to it. The altars are false, the originals being at the Newcastle Museum where the Mithraic exhibition is based. The Romans brought this religion over with them. The god Mithras was born in a cave under a star and is often referred to as a Sun God. It was a Roman Army religion (for men only) and was soon unpopular and made way for Christianity.

Sewingshields Crags: Leaving the fort, we continue to follow the road westwards. Opposite a cluster of trees the platform of Milecastle 32 (Carraw) can be detected. The scenes along the road are very fine on a clear day.

$2\frac{1}{2}$ miles west of Carrawbrough comes a highlight for any Wall walker. The road swings sharply south, and the Wall veers north to head for the crags, and so we finally leave the Military Road and the traffic. Old Hutton made mention of the occasion, 'But now I must quit this beautiful road, and the more beautiful scenes of cultivation, and enter upon the rude of Nature, and the wreck of Antiquity; for this grand military way bears to the left, and the Wall to the right'.

To indicate the turning, there is a signpost, 'Public Footpath—Sewingshields 1 mile'. The ditch and the Wall head for the higher ground, whereas the Vallum keeps to the low ground. There is no clear footpath at first, so keep to the high ground avoiding the low ditch which is the remains of the Vallum.

We immediately stumble into Turret 33b (Coesike) which is in good condition standing 6 courses high. Although we lose the Wall again it is now easy to follow as a mound of earth and stones remain. After climbing over a wall there is a second turret, 34a (Grindon West). Here we lose the ditch as the crags don't warrant its use.

Go past Sewingshields Farmhouse and through a

Carrawbrough Fort, The Mithraic Temple. (Reproduced by permission Northumberland National Parks Committee).

'nick'. On the far side is a wall. Follow this up the hill to some stepping stones over the wall leading through a small wood. Coming out on the opposite side a footpath continues to Sewingshield Crags, rising to 1,068 ft. Several pieces of Wall including Turret 35a are seen leading up to the summit which commands fine views incorporating Broomlee Lough ahead.

Busy Gap: We soon come to a gap in the crags known as Busy Gap where the ditch reappears to cover this low dip. Despite this extra defence, this 'nick' is famous for its many battles and frequent raiders, hence its name.

Continuing along the Wall, go over King's Hill and Kennet Crags leading past a small plantation. The Wall now comes back in all its fullness and leads down to a gateway discovered in 1856, and which is the best example of such today. The Wall takes you across the Knag Burn and up to the famous Housesteads Fort.

Right: Housesteads Fort, the latrine. (Ian Penney)

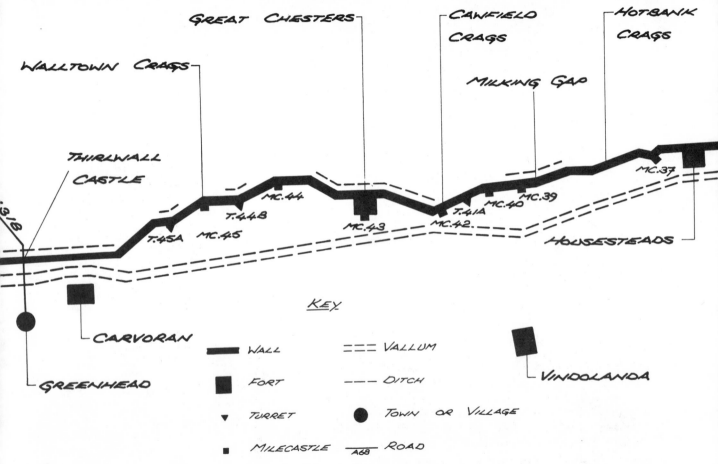

WALLTOWN CRAGS

GREAT CHESTERS

CAWFIELD CRAGS

HOTBANK CRAGS

MILKING GAP

THIRLWALL CASTLE

MC.37

MC.44

T.44B

MC.39

MC.40

T.41A

T.45A   MC.45

MC.43

MC.42.

HOUSESTEADS

3/8

CARVORAN

GREENHEAD

VINDOLANDA

KEY

⬛ WALL   ≡≡≡ VALLUM

⬛ FORT   --- DITCH

▼ TURRET   ● TOWN OR VILLAGE

■ MILECASTLE   A68 ROAD

3. Housesteads - Greenhead

Housesteads Fort: Housesteads is the most visited Roman site in Britain. It is attractively positioned on the crest of the Great Whin Sill with excellent views in all directions. It is the best surviving fort, and in each direction it is favoured with miles of Wall Country.

The Romans called the fort Vercovicium, meaning 'hilly place', and it covered an area of around 5 acres. Housesteads was constructed between A.D.125 and 128, and would have housed as many as a thousand infantrymen. The fort, however, experienced few battles, and by about A.D.400 many soldiers were made redundant, leaving only a couple of hundred men to 'hold the fort'.

All the fort walls are evident with the 4 gateways clearly visible. An impressive sight is the famous latrine, located in the south-east corner. Also the granaries are unusual to the eye, with the pillars in position that once supported the wooden floors allowing air to circulate underneath to keep the corn dry. The museum is situated south-west of the fort, and has many interesting finds from the fort and surrounding area.

Housesteads Crags and Milecastle: We leave Housesteads by the north-west angle, and start on one of the most exciting walks along the Wall. It is full of picturesque scenery, and it is possible to walk along the well-preserved way for miles on end. William Hutton was not as lucky in 1801. He says that the Wall was there, 'but miserably broken, and continues in the same style six or seven miles, a heap of rubbish!' Today, much more has been excavated and the Department of the Environment lovingly cares for what remains.

Immediately we are taken through Housesteads Wood and along Housesteads Crags to Milecastle 37 (Housesteads). It is one of the Wall's best preserved milecastles, standing as high as 21 courses.

Cuddy's and Hotbank Crags: The Wall then continues over Cuddy's Crags, and on the descent you arrive at an abrupt halt. You are left with an alternative: either climb down the rocky face or take an easier way by descending farther westwards. Having a large rucksack with me, and placing some value upon my life, I took to the latter. I looked up Old Hutton again to see how the old timer went on: 'I had now the severe task of creeping up rocks, and climbing stone walls, not well adapted to a man who has lost the activity of youth'.

Overlooking the Wall at Highshield Crags, taking in Crag Lough. (Ian Penney.)

At the foot of the hill is Rapishaw Gap where the Pennine Way has travelled down from the Scottish Border to join us in the walk over to Greenhead. We immediately rise up Hotbank Crags overlooking Greenlee Lough, and to the north-east the Cheviot Hills can be made out.

Descending Hotbank Crags we pass Hotbank Farm where we lose the Wall, but because of the low ground we gain the ditch again. This 'nick' is called Milking Gap, and is the site of a native settlement.

an undertaking. You can even climb on to the ramparts and take a Roman's-eye view of the enemy.

The whole tragedy of walking the Wall is that none of it stands at its original height, but here you have a glimpse of what the fortifications really looked like. The discoveries at Vindolanda mount up every year. Exciting finds have included leather footwear, pots and writing tablets. There is also a wealth of jewellery, weapons and all sorts of important evidence telling us more of how the Romans lived and worked. There is an informative museum which, along with the fort, is in the care of the Vindolanda Trust.

Vindolanda: It is at Milking Gap that I left the Wall once more to head for Vindolanda (our next 'fort of call') which lies 2 miles south of the Wall. A footpath by the side of Bradley Burn leads down to the Military Road (B6318). Take a field-path past High Shield Farm down to the fort. Before arrival you cross the Stanegate, on which a Roman milestone still stands in its original position.

The English name for the fort is Chesterholm, but the Roman name of Vindolanda remains the more popular. It is presently the active site of modern excavation work and certainly a call not to be missed.

Along with Roman remains that have been dug up, there is a reconstruction of the Wall (both stone and turf) from which you can comprehend the vastness of the Rom-

Highshield and Peel Crags: Back on the Wall we continue west from Milking Gap over a stile and through a wood on the banks of Crag Lough. We rise again over Highshield Crags where the cliff edge is very steep and drops more than 50ft. to the Lough below. The walk along this section is like one long roller coaster, going over crags and dropping into low 'nicks'.

We then arrive at Milecastle 39 (Castle Nick) which is in good condition and stands 6 courses high. A field wall continues the line of the Wall to the next 'nick' called Cat Stairs. We then climb up on to Peel Crags where the Wall, not in its best condition, joins us again. From here fine views can again be taken, in particular the view back along Hadrian's Wall. Then we arrive at Peel Gap. If this is a roller coaster we have been along, then here is the big dipper! We approach an almost sheer 100ft. drop where the Wall vanishes and wooden steps have been inserted for our convenience. Here, even the experienced walker cannot fail to break into a sweat and stop to catch his breath. At the foot of this hill is a lane leading to Twice Brewed, and the Once Brewed Youth Hostel.

The Wall arrives back in good condition just beyond the site of Milecastle 40, which itself is not easily placed. The summit of Winshield Crags is marked by an Ordnance Survey Triangulation Station. From here the Wall gently guides us down the west side of the crags and over another field wall with stepping stones.

I couldn't help but praise Hadrian here, for although he made it tough going for the walker, his Wall couldn't have been in a better position, commanding the whole countryside for miles around. It must have looked terrifying at full height.

Winshield Crags: From Peel Gap, we head north and then west past Steel Rigg car park. Here it is possible again to walk on the Wall until a lane leading to the car park is reached. Continue over the lane where stepping-stones allow easy access to the next field. The ditch remains prominent, but Hadrian's Wall is substituted by a field wall which no doubt used the former as its source.

Keep the wall to your right and pass through a gate which will lead you steeply up to Winshield Crags. This is the highest point of the walk at 1,230ft. above sea level. From here the high peaks of the Lake District can be seen with Cross Fell to the south. Looking east along the Wall our path over the crags from Sewingshields can be easily seen. Below where we stand the Vallum is apparent running adjacent to the B6318.

Cawfield Crags and Milecastle: The Emperor leads us down to a road, after which Turret 41a is detected. From this point it is possible to walk on the Wall all the way over Cawfield Crags. It is a lovely walk, not as steep as the previous crags but commanding lovely views.

After the descent we arrive at a well-preserved milecastle, Cawfields Milecastle 42, which was excavated in 1848. Just past the milecastle is a kissing gate which leads to a picnic area. We cannot get any farther along the Wall here because quarrying has removed the line, and any access to it is impossible. So we descend to the car park at the picnic spot which is nicely situated by the side of Cawfields Reservoir.

Cawfield Milecastle (42), excavated in 1848. (Colin Walker—Pendyke Publications.)

We pick up the line of the Wall again by going through the car park to the road. Turn left, then right and on the left hand side of this lane some stepping stones will be seen leading into a field. Go over, keeping the stone wall to your right. We see nothing of Hadrian's handywork here, although if you peep over the field wall you will see traces of the ditch which has reappeared, as the Wall can no longer rely on its natural defences.

Continue in this north-westerly direction, passing from field to field and using stepping-stones in the field walls. As you pass a farm wander slightly westwards away from your course into the centre of the field, where stepping-stones again will be found in the wall.

Drawing of the vaulted entrance to the strongroom at Great Chesters Fort. (John Schofield.)

Great Chesters: Hadrian's Wall now appears as a grassy mound of stones, as though it is trying to push its way up to show everybody where it is. Continue to climb from one field to another, and just after a small plantation a small section of Wall is seen.

It is here that we arrive at the site of Great Chesters Fort. You will be glad of this reminder, for I walked past it before I realized that I had done so. As you can gather there is little to see. Like Housesteads (if you dare compare the two), it lies completely south of the Wall but covers a smaller area of 3 acres on the site of the demolished Milecastle 43.

If you have time to waste, you can walk round finding the occasional rampart and blocking walls. The only striking feature is the vaulted entrance to the strongroom located in the centre of the field. One or two other aspects can be detected if you are willing to plough your way through nettles and make friends with a bull who by now is weighing up every move you make. To sum up, Greatchesters is one of the disappointments of the Wall, and hardly worth going out of your way to see.

The Nine Nicks of Thirlwall: As we continue west we see the Narrow Wall, which has not been built on the Broad Foundation as previously seen. There doesn't seem to be any reason for this parting of company, unless the base of the Broad Wall was unsuitable here. The two, however, make friends at Cockmount Hill Wood.

The ditch on the right of the Wall is again plain, and the Military Way to our left is quite distinct. After leaving Cockmount Hill Wood, there is a gate, on the west post of which stands a milestone which once stood on the Military Way. The Wall gradually leads up the side of a hill and at times is better seen standing on the opposite side of it looking at the north side.

After passing the site of Milecastle 44 (Allolee), we enter the first of the 'Nine Nicks of Thirlwall'. They are consecutive gaps in the crags on a smaller scale than between Sewingshields and Cawfield Crags. Today only seven nicks remain as quarrying has eliminated the other two.

In each of the three nicks we are approaching, the ditch has been dug to guard the lower ground. After the second nick we rise to Mucklebank Crag, 860ft. high, which contains an excellent turret, 44b (Mucklebank). The north and west sides of the turret are recessed into the Wall, and it stands 7 courses high. We drop into the third depression, 'Walltown Nick', which is wider than the others and climbs up steeply to the site of Milecastle 45 (Walltown). Old Hutton, 'found the ascent so difficult that I sometimes was obliged to crawl on all fours'. Despite the difficulties in walking this stretch it is a very pleasant walk, presenting fine views from the summits.

Walltown Crags: Along Walltown Crags we follow the Wall, which has been kept in good condition until the Greenhead Quarry intervenes. At the fence turn left and round the quarry which brings you to the finest stretch of Wall to be seen along the crags today. It often rises to 12 courses high and dips spectacularly into the fifth 'nick'.

This section is lovingly cared for by the Department of the Environment and incorporates an important turret, 45a (Walltown Crags East). Excavations in 1959 showed that this was built prior to the Wall as a signal tower, and only later was the Wall built into it. This is no doubt the reason why it lies 100 yards short of the usual marked distance.

Again industry has denied us more Wall, for we soon arrive at a further incursion of the Greenhead Quarry. At the fence turn left, and a footpath leads down to a lane. Turn right, and the lane leads on to another minor road.

Carvoran: On the opposite side of the road, and to the south-west, is the site of Carvoran, the 11th fort along the Wall. It was situated at a good vantage point on the junction of Stanegate and the Maiden Way. Although Camden found the ruins 'very evident' in 1599, nothing worth seeing remains now. The fort measured $3\frac{1}{2}$ acres, but what lies within those limits is not wholly known. Many finds have been made here, however–none more exciting than the discovery of a Roman dry-measure found in 1915, and which is exhibited in the Chesters Museum.

So at the junction of the two lanes mentioned above, turn right and in a field on the left a small section of the Wall will be seen. Go past the Wall and over a field wall following the line of the ditch. Keep the ditch on the left and go over another field wall which then leads through the field and down past a farm. Go through a wooden gate, remembering, of course, to close it behind you.

Left: The ruins of Thirlwall Castle, a 14th Century castle built with stones from Hadrian's Wall, where King Edward I is said to have stayed on September 20th, 1306. (Colin Walker—Pendyke Publications).

Thirlwall Castle: The footpath leads along the side of a field and over a footbridge spanning the River Tipalt. On the right we have Thirlwall Castle. Thirlwall means 'through the Wall', as the castle is built in a gap through Hadrian's Wall. It is not Roman, however; it was built in the 14th century using stones from the Wall. It is attractively set on a hillock by the River Tipalt, but it is now in a sad state of ruin. Even Old Hutton in 1801 claims that it was 'far gone in decay'.

There is a popular story which says that Edward I stayed here on September 20th, 1306, on his last journey to the north.

The path leads us once more to the B6318. If you turn left here, you will come to Greenhead ($\frac{1}{4}$ mile) where the Pennine Way takes leave of us and heads south for Alston and the Pennines, whilst we must continue westwards towards the Solway Coast and our destination.

Right: The Wall at Walltown Crags, where it has to avoid a dolerite outcrop. (Colin Walker—Pendyke Publications.)

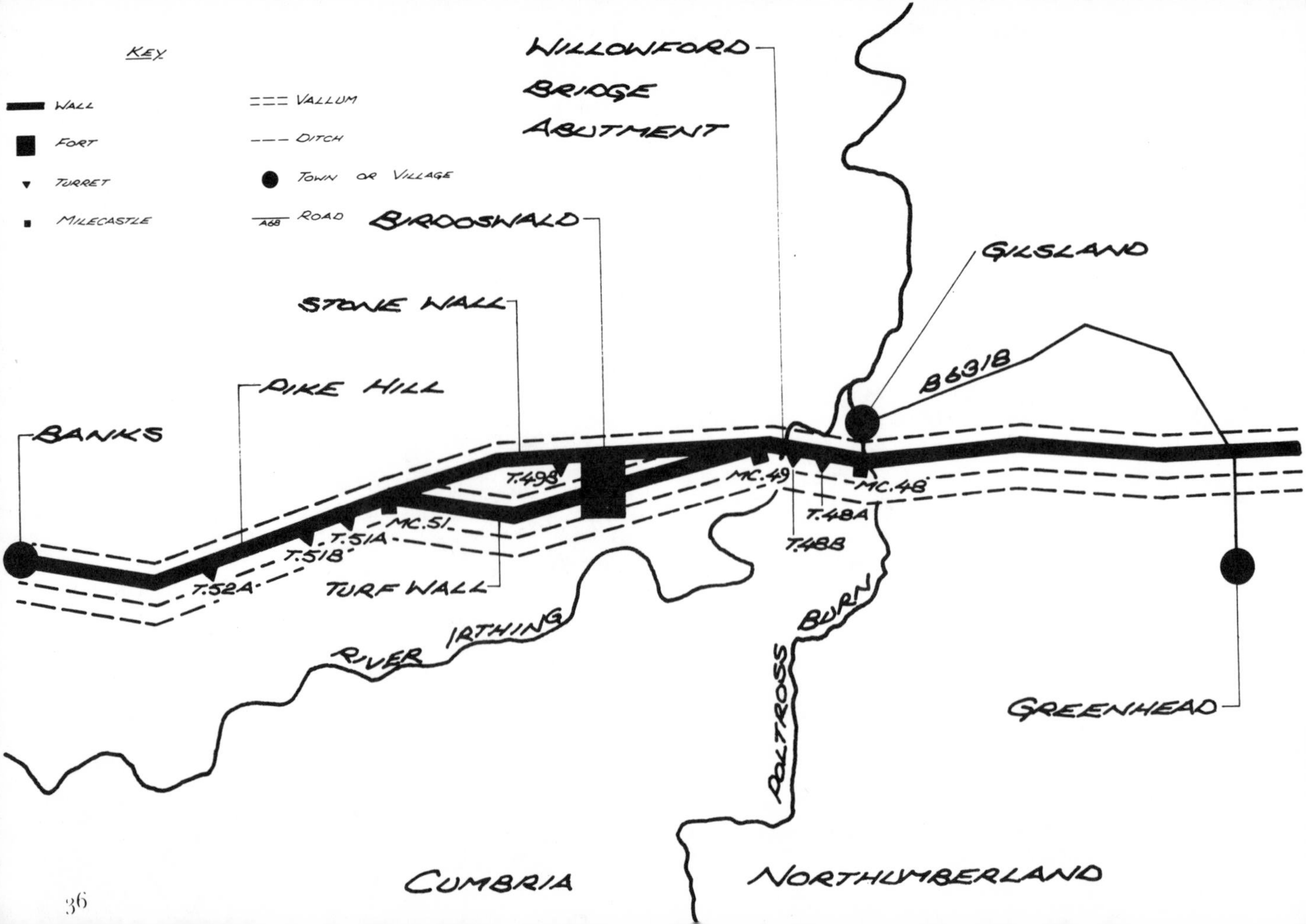

KEY

▬	WALL	≡	VALLUM
■	FORT	- - -	DITCH
▼	TURRET	●	TOWN OR VILLAGE
▪	MILECASTLE	A68	ROAD

WILLOWFORD BRIDGE ABUTMENT

BIRDOSWALD

GILSLAND

STONE WALL

PIKE HILL

B6318

BANKS

T.49B

MC.49

MC.48

T.48A

T.48B

MC.51

T.51A

T.51B

T.52A

TURF WALL

RIVER IRTHING

POLTROSS BURN

GREENHEAD

CUMBRIA

NORTHUMBERLAND

36

4. Greenhead - Banks

Greenhead: The crags and the real 'Wall Country' are now behind us, and the countryside becomes more undulating as we head for the Irthing Valley. Greenhead is a small village, just a cluster of houses really, but it is a busy concern lying on the junction of the A69 and the B6318. It was at Greenhead in 1797 that Sir Walter Scott, at the age of 26, met his wife to be, Charlotte Carpenter. And here it was that he penned his poem: 'To a Lady, with Flowers from a Roman Wall'.

'Take these flowers which, purple waving, On the ruined rampart grew, Where, the sons of freedom braving, Rome's imperial standard flew.

Warriors from the breach of danger Pluck no longer laurels there; They but yield the passing stranger Wild-flower wreaths for Beauty's hair'.

The village also prides itself with a 19th century church which has an attractive slender spire.

The B6318 takes us back up to the line of the Wall. On the left hand side of the road a chunk of the Wall can be seen. It is here that the Wall continues westwards to Gilsland, though only the ditch and Vallum are evi-dent today.

Gilsland: The course heads over a golf course and private land, and so we must take the B6318 into Gilsland, the line of the Wall running to our left. If any enthusiast, however, wishes to follow the Wall exactly, a map and compass will be essential, as much of the path is undefined. Nevertheless, there are good stretches of the ditch, par-ticularly after Gap Farm.

Gilsland is a lovely village situated where the Poltross Burn runs into the River Irthing. A beautiful walk can be taken up the Irthing Valley, leaving Gilsland by the side of the Bath House. It is along this walk that the famous 'Popping Stone' is located jutting out of the river. This is where Sir Walter Scott is said to have 'popped' the question to Charlotte Carpenter, which led to their marriage in Carlisle Cathedral on Christmas Eve, 1797.

Poltross Burn Milecastle: At Gilsland there is, in my opinion, the best milecastle along the Wall; 48, Poltross Burn. There are two ways of access from the village. The first is by the side of the railway bridge as signposted. Alternatively, go up a track by the side of the Co-op. Turn first left along a footpath leading up the railway embankment. Go through the subway and turn left. The path leads to a wooden bridge over the Poltross Burn, and up to the milecastle. As we cross the footbridge we leave Northumberland, and from here onwards the Wall takes up residence in the county of Cumbria (formerly Cumberland).

The milecastle is under the guardianship of the De-partment of the Environment, and although the whole outline is not visible it contains more internal features than any other. It measures 70ft. (north – south) and 60ft. 9ins. (west – east), and the walls are set at the Broad Gauge. The 9½ft. gateways are clearly seen and the remains of a flight of steps are situated in the north-east corner. In the north-west angle are the remains of an oven, and burn marks can still be seen.

The Romanway: Leaving Milecastle 48 you go over a stile opposite the north-west corner of the milecastle. You then go over another stile which brings you across the railway lines and into the grounds of 'Romanway'. Although running through private ground the owners, Mr. & Mrs. Ron Dawkins, don't mind Wall walkers at all, apart from those who stare through their windows. If time allows they will even be ready to tell you that this stretch of Wall is one of the finest examples of the Narrow on Broad type, and it is kept in fine condition by the English Heritage men.

The house itself is built from stones out of the Wall, although covered by modern bricks, and outside the front door two Roman altars stand. One of them is uninscribed, the other is dedicated to Jupiter.

Willowford Wall: Across the Brampton Road, access is gained to a good stretch of Wall leading to the Willowford Bridge Abutment. There is a good 100 yard piece of Wall before it changes direction, keeping the meandering River Irthing on its right. Here we have a fine turret, 48a Willowford East, standing 10 courses high.

A little farther on, we see that the ditch is well preserved, and accompanies the Wall to Turret 48b, Willowford West, which is not as well preserved as its eastern brother. The northern wall stands 9 courses high, but the south wall has been reduced to its bottom course.

Willowford Bridge Abutment: We now arrive at a farm and for 200 yards the Wall runs through land adjoining

it. The tenant farmer makes a small charge for access to the abutments.

It is a lovely stretch of Wall standing 6ft. high, and marches triumphantly down to the River Irthing. Here a bridge once stood to carry the Wall, and later the Military Way, over the river. As at Chesters the river has changed course and has left remains of the eastern abutment for all to see. It is not as grand as Chesters, but part of the 20ft. square tower remains.

Harrow's Scar: We are now faced with a difficulty; to cross the river and climb up the steep western bank to save a 4 mile detour back through Gilsland. William Hutton had a hard time here, 'I had this river to cross, and this mountain to ascend; but did not know how to perform either. I effected a passage over the river by the assistance of stones as large as myself, sometimes in, and sometimes out; but with difficulty reached the summit of the precipice by a zig-zag line, through the brambles, with a few scratches'.

I was lucky to wade over the river during a dry spell using the same stones as Hutton used. The ascent up the hill is easier today as there is a footpath with wooden blocks recessed into the bank. The path leading up this hill is known as Harrow's Scar and arrives at Milecastle 49 which bears the same name. Along with its predecessor (M/C 48), it is one of the finest along the Wall, standing 7 courses high.

This is an ideal vantage point to have a milecastle, most noteworthy is the view looking back towards

Gilsland. Excavation work found part of a Turf Wall milecastle, as it was west of the Irthing crossing that the Turf Wall was built. The Turf and Stone Walls here take separate courses, the former running south of the latter.

Birdoswald: Leaving the milecastle we go through a kissing gate and follow a well preserved stretch of Narrow Wall. It is along here that some Roman inscriptions have been found on the south face of the Wall, and they have been indicated by lead arrows inserted in the lower course pointing up to the markings. In Roman times this area was boggy and drainage channels can still be seen in the Wall.

Hadrian's Wall terminates at a lane which leads to Birdoswald Fort, the road itself taking away the Wall. The original Turf Wall kept south and joined the fort at its eastern gateway, but the Stone Wall heads for the north-east angle.

Birdoswald Fort has seen some major developments in recent years. The farm which stands on the site, together with 150 acres of adjoining land, was acquired by Cumbria County Council in 1984. Thanks to a £¼ million grant from British Nuclear Fuels important excavation work took place from 1987 to 1992. Although the East Gate still remains the best preserved aspect of the fort, there is now much more to see. Indeed, Birdoswald is now a unique tourist attraction as all the components of the Roman frontier system – Brick Wall, Turf Wall, Fort, Milecastle – can be found here.

Along with the major excavation work, the site has developed to cater for the increased number of visitors it attracts – presently in excess of 23,000 per year. Car park, toilets, shop, exhibition area with audio-visual presentations and an attractive cafe have been provided. I was impressed that Birdoswald, which has English Heritage as its guardian, has conserved the atmosphere of the site. Because there is work going on here it is a 'living site' with always something new to see.

Although Birdoswald will have its work cut out to compete with Housesteads Fort, there is a lot going for it. It is very accessible (excellent for disabled visitors) with the road running right alongside the main entrance. It is also one of the most picturesque settings along the whole of the Hadrian's Wall corridor. Walk southwards out of the fort and you come to a lovely wooded picnic spot overlooking the Irthing Gorge. Open from 1st April to 31st October, the modest charge for admission includes a self-guided trail leaflet.

Birdoswald Turret: Leaving the fort, we have a continuation of the Narrow Wall for a third of a mile, when it comes to an abrupt halt. The country here is very rural with farms and cottages, and is most enjoyable to walk. To the south, grand views of the Irthing Valley can be seen, and occasionally in the fields near to us parts of the Turf Wall can be detected as mounds of earth.

Along this stretch we find Turret 49b, Birdoswald Turret, standing up to 9 courses high in its north wall. The lane is now robbed of the Stone Wall, the road itself being the main culprit. We go past Appletrees Farm, and on the site of Milecastle 51, the Turf Wall ditch can be seen coming in and joining the Narrow Wall ditch which has been running to our right.

From this point the two Walls converge and run together down to the village of Banks. The Vallum on the south side of the road is very clear, and brings us to Turret 51a, Piper Sike. It is well preserved, standing up to 6 courses high. A better turret, though, is found in 51b, Lea Hill. It is a good example of a Turf Wall turret still seen at 8 courses high. The Narrow Stone Wall can be seen abutting it, and the doorway is particularly striking.

Pike Hill: As we continue westwards down the lane the view to the south still commands interest, and on the horizon the Lakeland Peaks are prominent. It is on this vantage point that we have the remains of a Roman signal tower called Pike Hill. It was similar in size to a turret, although the road has severed most of it. Actually it was built before the Wall, about A.D.122, and was occupied until the late 4th century.

A footpath leads down to a car park and on the opposite side is Turret 52a, Banks East. This has survived better than the Piper Sike and Lea Hill turrets mentioned above. It stands 12 courses high and has a small section of Narrow Wall joining it. The English Heritage has taken all this section under its wing.

Right: Birdoswald Fort, showing the East Gate. On each side of the gate there is a tower about the size of a turret.

LD.53.　EAST GATE. BIRDOSWALD. GILSLAND.

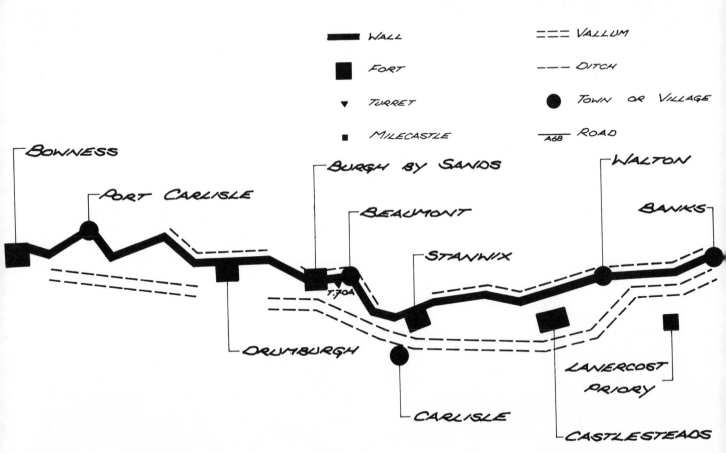

Key

Wall — Vallum ===
Fort ■ Ditch ---
Turret ▼ Town or Village ●
Milecastle ■ Road A68

Bowness
Port Carlisle
Burgh by Sands
Beaumont
Walton
Banks
Stanwix
Drumburgh
T.70A
Carlisle
Lanercost Priory
Castlesteads

5. Banks - Bowness

Banks: A $\frac{1}{4}$ mile west of the L.Y.C. Museum we arrive at a cluster of houses collectively called Banks. As you enter, a minor road will be seen on the right. Turn along it, and at the junction with another road turn left. Immediately on the right you will see a sign: 'Public Footpath Walton'. Half way up Hare Hill, as it is called, in a field on the right will be seen a piece of Wall standing 9ft. 10ins. high, the highest stretch of Wall to be seen today. Old William Hutton recalled, 'I viewed this relick with admiration; I saw no part higher; it was within two feet of the battlements'.

Along this footpath you pass a white house and then a stile takes you into a field. Pass the farm, and at the north-west corner of the field a gate will be seen, where access is gained to the next field. We are now virtually walking on the Wall, although there is no trace of it and only the ditch remembers Hadrian. The path leads over Craggle Hill where good views exist to the south.

Lanercost Priory: Proceed along the footpath and over stiles until a junction of two paths is reached with cattle grids at each entrance. To continue along the Wall go straight ahead over a footbridge.

By turning left over the cattle grid you will be led to the beautiful Lanercost Priory. It was founded in 1166 and the nave is still used as a church today. It was built from stones out of Hadrian's Wall—no wonder little survives in this part. Unfortunately the Wall was too often used as a 'made to measure' quarry, and places like Thirlwall Castle and Lanercost Priory made the most of it. Edward I was a frequent visitor to Lanercost and indeed spent his last winter here.

Dovecote Bridge: The footbridge mentioned above —and which has been covered by trees—leads over a small burn to a field. The footpath is not clearly defined, but make a bee-line to the far side where a stile will be seen leading to the next field. Go over the stile and left, keeping the hedge on your right. This brings you out on a lane. The line of the Wall, not visible here, continues in the field opposite, but access is not possible.

We continue by turning right (north) along the lane, then first left signposted Walton. A mile along this road we go over a hump bridge called Dovecote Bridge. Just over the bridge the last remaining piece of Wall can be seen. The signpost, unusually, reads 'Hadrian's Wall', and not 'Roman Wall', as do all the other signs we have seen. The Wall itself is unusual as it is the only surviving piece that was built of sandstone, presenting a deep red hue.

Walton: From here we enter the lovely village of Walton. The name is thought by some to be derived from 'Wall Town'; some locals pronounce it 'Watton'. The sandstone church in the village has an unusual pyramid-shaped spire, and claims to have the heaviest bell for miles.

Go through Walton past the Centurian Inn (formerly the Black Bull). This may also have been the 'Cow and Boot' where William Hutton stayed the night when he visited the village. The landlady refused to take more than a few pence from the old man, even though he had laid down two shillings. Hutton wrote with conviction, 'When a man serves me with his best in time of need, he merits my money and my thanks'.

From the Inn take the second turning on the right. The dirt track leads past some houses and through a gate to a field. Go through, keeping on the south side of the field. Continue through another gate which brings you to Sandysike Farm. The farm is built mainly from Hadrian's Wall, and in one of the farm walls a stone with a Roman inscription can be found. The farmer said he didn't know what it meant, but a man from Sheffield was coming up the following week to look at it.

Castlesteads: Leave the farm by the same entrance and opposite there is a cattle grid and a path which leads down to a country lane. Before the lane is reached, on the right you will see a large house called Castlesteads. This is the site of the next fort on the Wall bearing the same name.

Nothing today remains at Castlesteads, although some Roman remains are found in the grounds of the house. Uxellodunum, as the Romans called the fort, lies south of the Wall and is not connected to it as most Wall forts are. The lane leads down to the A6071, and turning left will bring you to Brampton. A right turn leads to Newtown which lies upon the line of the Wall. Many walkers will go to Brampton and take a 'bus or train to Carlisle, as nothing at all remains from here. I personally recommend that approach, as the walk is generally disinteresting and passes Carlisle Airport and the M6.

Those wishing to walk all the way for the sake of prestige, or as an endurance test, should leave Newtown for Oldwall, which lies to the north of the airport, then go on through Walby and join the B6264 into Carlisle.

Stanwix: The B6264 goes through Stanwix, where the Romans built their next fort on the Wall to guard the River Eden. It was an important position, lying on the main western route from Scotland, and here Hadrian built his largest fort extending over 9 acres and capable of housing 1000 men, although when used as a cavalry fort it would only hold half that number. Unfortunately nothing of the fort is visible today.

A number of remains found here and along this western sector are to be found in the Tullie House Museum in Carlisle

Tullie House: No walker along the Wall should pass through Carlisle without paying a visit to the Tullie House Museum. There has been a museum in Carlisle since 1836 and Tullie House, a Jacobean mansion, has been the permanent home for exhibiting border collections since the 1890's. Exactly a century later the old buildings were refurbished and a new wing built at a cost of £5,000,000.

Although the museum covers man's occupation of these parts over many periods, there is an excellent section devoted to the Roman era in general and Hadrian's Wall in particular. It is designed to be an interpretive centre. Young and old alike will enjoy climbing up a reconstruction of part of the Wall giving you the 'feel' of being on the front line.

There are many fine exhibits, too. Altars, statues as well as smaller items to inspect. The new museum has been well designed and includes a shop, restaurant and a film theatre. It is situated next to Castle Way (A595) just across from the Castle.

From Carlisle take the A595 out of the city, passing Carlisle Castle and following the B5307, turning right past an infirmary. A mile along this road there is a minor road going off at an angle where a telephone box is situated. Go along here, and just before the electric pylons the Vallum can be detected running along the river's edge where the Wall took up residence.

Kirkandrews on Eden: Turn right then left over a hump bridge and through the village of Kirkandrews on Eden. The Wall here ran north of the village, whilst the Vallum took its own course on the south side of it. This stretch of Wall to Bowness has been confusing for archaeologists, for whereas the Wall generally has been taking a straight course, there are here, in the space of 14 miles, 34 changes in direction. It is hard to say why this is so, but one theory is that the water levels were much different in Roman times and the Wall had continually to steer clear of them.

Beaumont: From Kirkandrews on Eden take a right turn to Beaumont, the line of the Wall being to the north of the road while the Vallum cuts across through Monkhill. At Beaumont (pronounced Beemont) there stands a church elevated on a knoll, and on the site of Turret 70a. The church is mainly built from Hadrian's Wall, and the Wall was actually found in the grounds.

Burgh by Sands: From Beaumont take the road heading south-west for Monkhill. Turn right where we leave the Wall and follow the Vallum into Burgh by Sands which housed the Roman fort Aballava, meaning Appletrees. The fort covered nearly 5 acres and ecompassed Turret 71b. The church at Burgh (pronounced Bruff) is almost entirely built from the Wall and dates back to the late thirteenth or early fourteenth century.

A signpost in the village points to the King Edward I monument which is situated out in the Burgh marshes. The monument is supposed to be erected where the King breathed his last on his way to Scotland. It is fitting that we should meet Edward again; we first made acquaintances at Thirlwall Castle and again at Lanercost, and now with our destination in sight he takes his leave of us forever.

As we leave Burgh the Wall is to our right and the Vallum soon follows suit. The sand banks of the River Eden close fast upon us until we come almost upon the beach itself. With the Wall being between us and the estuary I would have thought that it would be in danger from flooding, but perhaps that wasn't such a threat in those days. What a sight the Wall must have looked from across the channel in Scotland!

Drumbrugh: Four miles west of Burgh we arrive at Drumburgh (pronounced Drumbuff) where the Romans built their fort, Congavata. It was ideally situated on a hill overlooking the flat countryside. Drumburgh has a castle which is really a manor house situated south of the village and built by Thomas, Lord Dacre, using Roman stones. The Rev. John Leland noted in his itinerary that at 'Drumbuygh. For the Wal ys very nere yt'.

As we continue westwards the road runs almost on the line of the Wall which zig-zags to Port Carlisle. The Vallum takes a straighter course through the village of Glasson.

Port Carlisle: Port Carlisle is but one street, but nevertheless a lovely spot. It was hoped, many years ago, to build up this cluster of houses to act as an important port linking with its big brother, Carlisle. Although a canal was built the venture never paid its way and ceased to function in 1853. Many houses round here were built from the Wall, and just before you leave the village Hesket House exhibits a Roman altar above the front door.

And so we leave Port Carlisle with excitement, knowing that the next village is the last stop on our walk from the Tyne.

Bowness on Solway: Just a mile and a half from Port Carlisle we walk into Bowness on Solway, the last fort on the Wall. Surprisingly it is the second largest fort on the Wall, covering more than 7 acres. I had been wondering why the Romans bothered about arming themselves with a Wall an such a large fort when the Solway acted as a natural defence, but I have been told (although I never tried it myself) that at low tide you can actually wade over into Scotland, and no doubt the Romans were concerned as to the opposite happening.

Again the fort is a good one, standing on a 50ft hill overlooking the surrounding flat ground. Standing on this hill today is a church, and opposite the church yard the bath house once stood. There was also a large Roman settlement here which was evacuated about A.D.365.

A signpost in the village pointed to the Solway Banks, where I soaked up the scenery and sunshine as I contemplated with pleasure my journey along Hadrian's Wall.

Bibliography

HANDBOOK TO THE ROMAN WALL by J. Collingwood Bruce, edited by Sir Ian Richmond. Published by Hindson, Newcastle-upon-Tyne. The standard guide for over a century, with a wealth of detailed information on every site.

THE HISTORY OF THE ROMAN WALL by William Hutton. Published by John Nichols, London, in 1802. Now out-of-print, you will be lucky to find a copy today even in the second-hand bookshops. A facsimile has been produced by Templer Books, York.

HADRIAN'S WALL, A PRACTICAL GUIDE TO THE VISIBLE REMAINS by R. W. Davies. Published by Eyewitness, Sunderland. A good guide, particularly for motorists.

A WALK ALONG THE WALL by Hunter Davies. Published by Quartet Books, London, in paperback. A well written account of the Wall and the people who live around it.

CORBRIDGE by Professor Eric Birley. The official Department of the Environment guide. Published by H.M.S.O.

CHESTERS by Professor Eric Birley. The official Department of the Environment guide. Published by H.M.S.O.

HOUSESTEADS by Professor Eric Birley. The official Department of the Environment guide. Published by H.M.S.O.

VINDOLANDA by the Site Director, Robin Birley. Published by Frank Graham, Newcastle-on-Tyne.

BIRDOSWALD by Peter Howard. Published by Cameo Books, Huddersfield.

ORDNANCE SURVEY map of Hadrian's Wall. 2 ins. to 1 mile. An excellent map showing all the visible remains (in black), and what used to be there (in red).

ORDNANCE SURVEY 1:50,000 maps. To cover the full length of the Wall you need:
SHEET 85 Carlisle & Solway Firth. SHEET 86 Haltwhistle and Bewcastle. SHEET 87 Hexham and Haltwhistle. SHEET 88 Tyneside.